String Explorer

A Journey into the Wonders of String Playing

Andrew Dabczynski • Richard Meyer • Bob Phillips

PIANO ACCOMPANIMENT
Book 1

This book contains piano accompaniments for every line of music in *String Explorer*, Book 1. The violin part from the student book is reproduced above each accompaniment.

In addition, optional piano accompaniments are included for the four period ensemble pieces, "Arco's Blues," and all Activity Page exercises in which students play their instrument.

Chord symbols are provided if you wish to improvise your own accompaniment part or choose to add guitar or other instruments.

The authors would like to thank Kim Kasabian, Tim Phillips, Greg Plumblee and Kate Westin for their help with the editorial development and production of this series.

Illustrations: John Kachik

Alfred

ISBN 0-7390-2501-5

UNIT 1

Activity 3: Open String Echoes

1. **Activity 4: Open String Blues** (pizz.)
   Activity 13: Open String Blues
   Activity 14: Open String Blues in Perfect Playing Position

UNIT 2

Ready, set, **BOW!**

2. Down, Up, Down, Up

3. Motorcycle, Stop, Stop

4. Down, Up, Down, Up

5. Motorcycle, Stop, Stop

Finger "Tips"

E-Z Does It

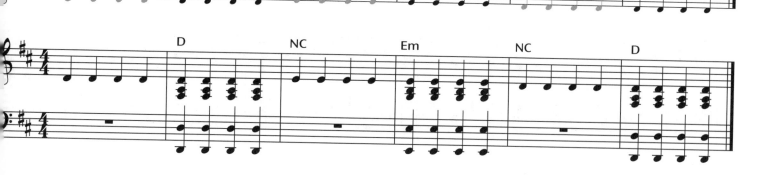

7. Second Rung

8. The D Ladder, Ascending

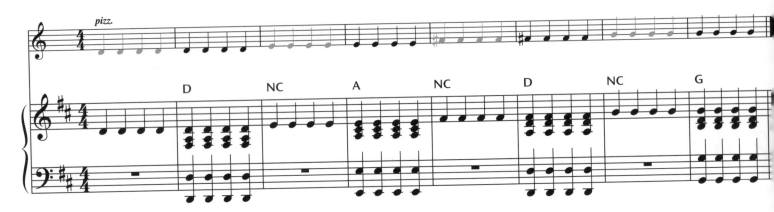

9. The D Ladder, Descending

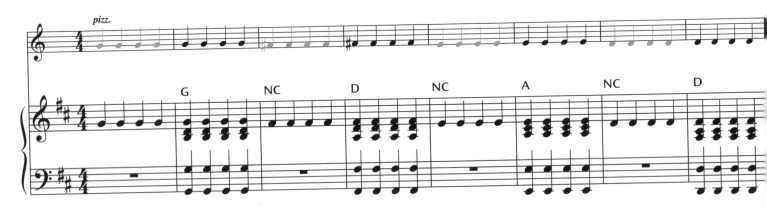

10. The D Ladder, Ascending and Descending

4

Putting It **Together**

11. Bowing the D Ladder

12. Motorcycles Stopping on the D Ladder

3. Hot Cross Buns

English Folk Song

5

UNIT 3
Ready, set, BOW!

14. Elevator Operator

15. Run Pony, Run Pony

16. Elevator Operator

17. Run Pony

Finger "Tips"

18. The A Ladder, Ascending

. The A Ladder, Descending

. The A Ladder, Ascending and Descending

Putting It **Together**

. Elevator Operator on the A Ladder

22. Ponies Running on the A Ladder

23. Lifting the Bow

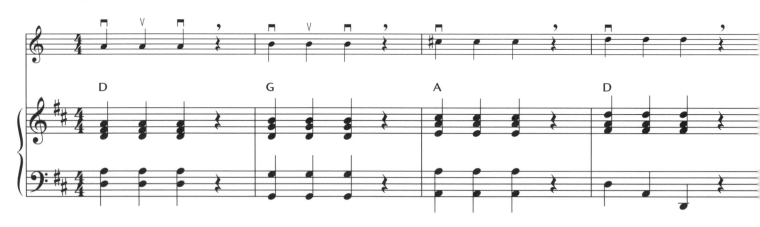

24. Mary Had a Little Lamb

English Folk So[ng]

Ready, set, **BOW!**

5. String to String

6. Crossing Over

Finger "Tips"

7. Pluckin' the D Scale

8. Pluckin' Down the D Scale

29. Exploring Intervals

Putting It **Together**

30. Bows and 'Cycles

1. Cycling Down the D Scale

2. Twinkle, Twinkle, Little Star

French Folk Song

33. Twinklin' the Spokes

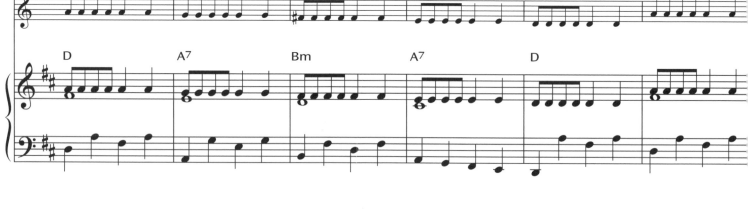

EXPLORING REPERTOIRE

4. Jingle Bells

J. S. Pierpont

35. Ode to Joy

Ludwig van Beethoven (1770–182

6. Chanukah, Chanukah

Israeli Folk Song

7. Are You Sleeping?

French Folk Song

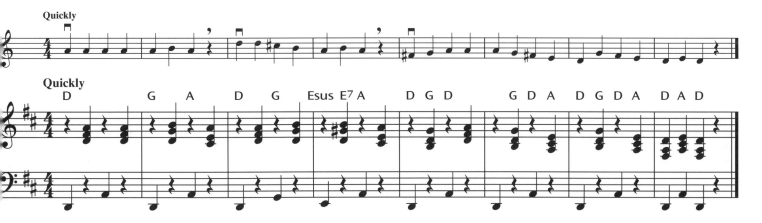

ACTIVITY PAGE 1

Exploring World Music: Polish Tatra Song

UNIT 5
Ready, set, **BOW!**

38. Beats and Rests

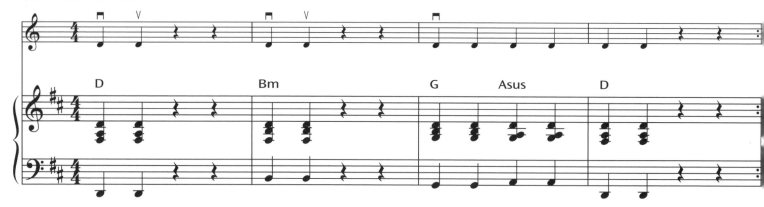

39. Rosalyn's Favorite

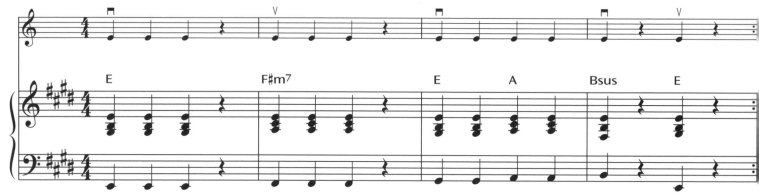

40. Resting and Lifting

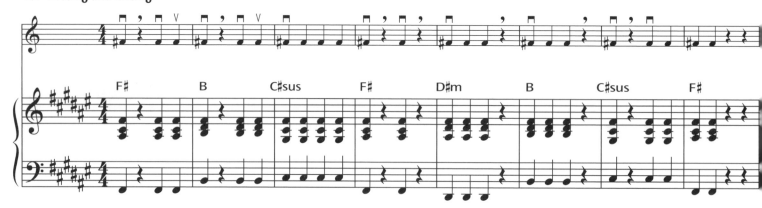

41. A Crop of Sugar Beats

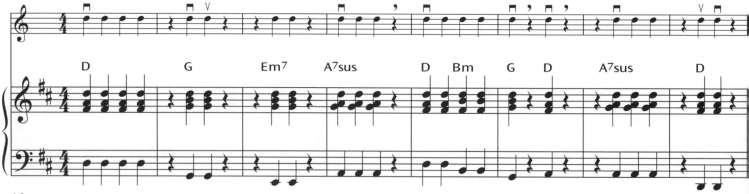

Finger "Tips"

2. Exploring D and E

43. Exploring F#

4. Walking Up and Back

5. Walking and Skipping

6. Heading Home

Putting It Together

47. Trial Run

48. Lift Off

49. Au claire de la lune

French Folk Song

50. Riding the Waves

51. Cuckoo Clock

52. Theme and Variations on Mary Had a Little Lamb

English Folk Song

53. Variation I: Inversion

54. Variation II: Jazz

UNIT 6

Ready, set, BOW!

55. Running Ponies on the Staff

56. Pony Runs Back

57. Two Endings

58. Motorcycles on the Elevator

Finger "Tips"

59. Exploring G

60. Exploring A

61. Riding the Rails

62. The Tunnel

63. Lake Shore Limited

21

Putting It **Together**

64. Climbing the Steps

65. Oats, Peas and Beans

American Folk Song

66. Huron Sunset

22

57. Theme and Variations on Ode to Joy

Ludwig van Beethoven (1770–1827)

68. Variation

UNIT 7

Ready, set, **BOW!**

69. Half and Half

70. Exploring Dynamics

71. Black and White

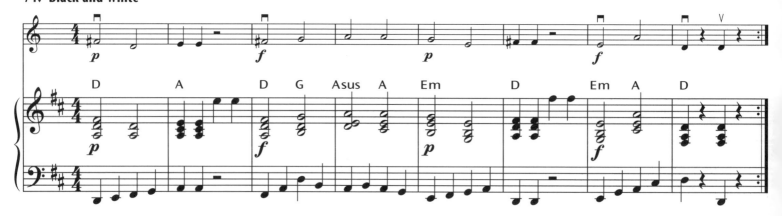

72. Forever Forte

Finger "Tips"

73. Base Camp

74. Almost There

75. The Summit

76. Steppes of A-sia

77. At the Ball Park

78. Jersey Shuffle

Putting It **Together**

79. Canyon Echoes

80. Mary's Lament

81. Bile Them Cabbage Down (Duet)

American Folk Song
and Fiddle Tune

82. Carmela

83. Fork and Spoon (Duet)

84. Arco's Quickstep

UNIT 8

Ready, set, BOW!

85. Starts and Stops

86. Exploring Slurs

87. Captain Hook

88. Exploring Staccato

89. Cactus and Molasses

Finger "Tips"

90. Exploring the D Major Scale

91. Exploring Arpeggios

92. Exploring Thirds

93. Antrim Hills

Putting It **Together**

94. Fancy London Bridge

English Folk Song

95. Hookuna Legato

96. Chester (Duet)

William Billings (1746–1800)

97. Can Can

Jacques Offenbach (1819–1880)

EXPLORING THE BAROQUE ERA

Brandenburg Concerto No. 5

Johann Sebastian Bach (1685–1750)

Arr. R. Meyer

Exploring Music Theory

Exploring Composition

Exploring World Music: Paso Doble

UNIT 9

Ready, set, BOW!

98. Three in a Measure

99. Slow Bow

100. Down, Up, Up

101. Rosalyn's Waltz

Finger "Tips"

102. Left-Hand Pizz.

103. Fourth-Finger A

104. Finger Mixer

Putting It Together

105. Drink to Me Only

English Folk Song

106. Barcarolle (Duet)

Jacques Offenbach (1819–1880)

107. Perpetual Motion

108. Minuet

Johann Sebastian Bach (1685–1750)

109. Swingin' Pizz. Swing the eighth notes!

Ready, set, BOW!

110. Exploring Dotted Quarters

111. Explorer March

112. Tradewinds

Finger "Tips"

113. The G Ladder

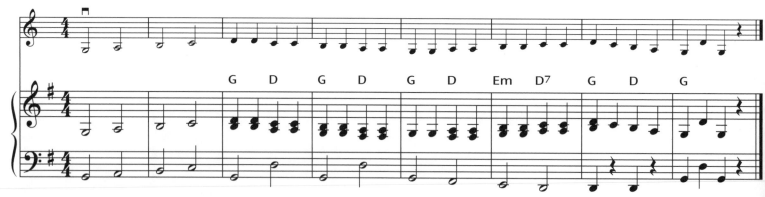

114. Exploring the G Major Scale

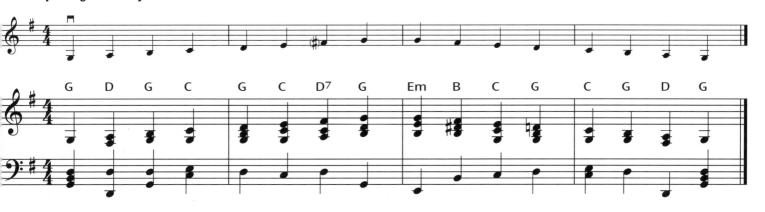

115. Dayenu

Israeli Folk Song

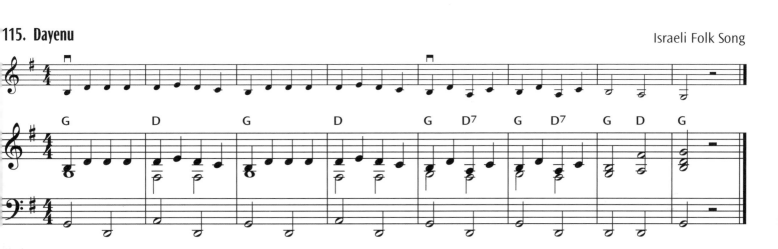

116. Exploring Arpeggios

117. Exploring Thirds

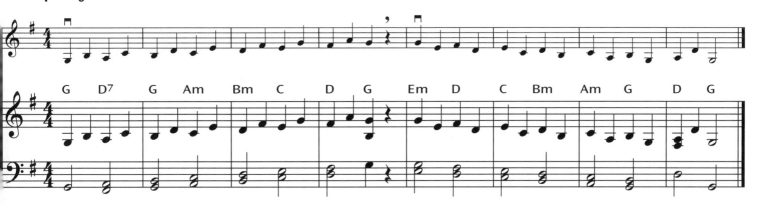

118. New World Symphony

Antonin Dvořák (1841–1904)

119. Judas Maccabaeus

George Frideric Handel (1685–1759)

120. We Gather Together

Dutch Hymn Tune

121. Oh! Susannah (Duet)

Stephen Collins Foster (1826–1864)

EXPLORING THE CLASSICAL ERA

Minuet (from Symphony No. 36)

Wolfgang Amadeus Mozart (1756–1791)
Arr. R. Meyer

ACTIVITY PAGE 3

Exploring Music Theory

Exploring Ear Training

Exploring Composition

Exploring World Music: Reminiscence of Lady Quin Er

UNIT 11

Ready, set, **BOW!**

122. Quarters, Halves, Wholes

123. Time Out

124. Ridin' the Strings

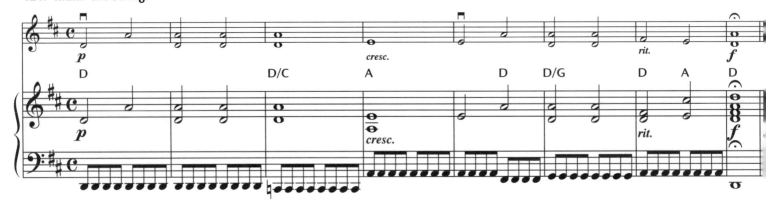

125. **Double Stop Shuffle** Swing the eighth notes!

Finger "Tips"

26. Exploring Naturals

27. The Natural Explorer

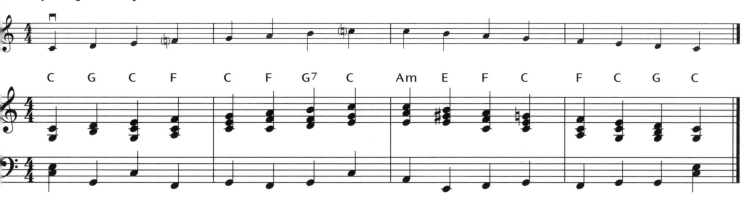

28. Exploring the C Major Scale

29. Exploring Arpeggios

130. Exploring Thirds

Putting It **Together**

131. Rigaudon

Henry Purcell (1659–1695)

132. Simple Gifts (Duet)

Shaker Hymn Tune

133. America

Patriotic

134. Old Joe Clark

American Folk Song

UNIT 12

Ready, set, **BOW!**

135. Exploring Accents

136. Freeze Tag

137. Bumps in the Road

138. Undersea Accents

Finger "Tips"

139. Exploring the E String

140. Further Exploration

141. Exploring the G Major Scale

142. Exploring Arpeggios

143. Exploring Thirds

Putting It Together

144. The Erie Canal

145. Swan Lake

Peter Ilyich Tchaikovsky (1840–1893)

146. Arirang (Duet)

Korean Folk Song

50

147. St. Anthony Chorale

Franz Joseph Haydn (1732–1809)

148. Shepherd's Hey

English-Australian Folk Song adapted by
Percy Aldridge Grainger (1882–1961)

EXPLORING THE ROMANTIC ERA

March of the Meistersingers

Richard Wagner (1813–1883)
Arr. R. Meyer

ACTIVITY PAGE 4

Exploring Ear Training

Exploring Composition

Exploring Improvisation: Cool Cross Buns

Exploring World Music: Apache Melody

UNIT 13

Ready, set, BOW!

149. Poppin' Bows

150. Dashes and Dots

151. William Tell Overture

Gioacchino Rossini (1792–1868)

Finger "Tips"

52. Exploring F Naturals and the C String

153. Further Exploration

54. Exploring the C Major Scale

155. Exploring Arpeggios

156. Exploring Thirds

157. Un Elefante

Mexican Folk Song

158. Russian Folk Song

Adapted by Peter Ilyich Tchaikovsky (1840–1893)

59. March in C

Johann Sebastian Bach (1685–1750)

60. The Victors

Louis Elbel

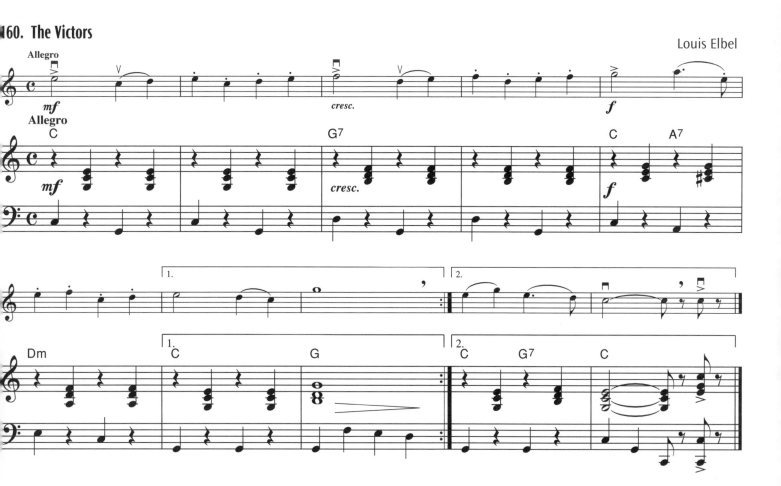

UNIT 14

Ready, set, BOW!

161. Exploring Syncopation

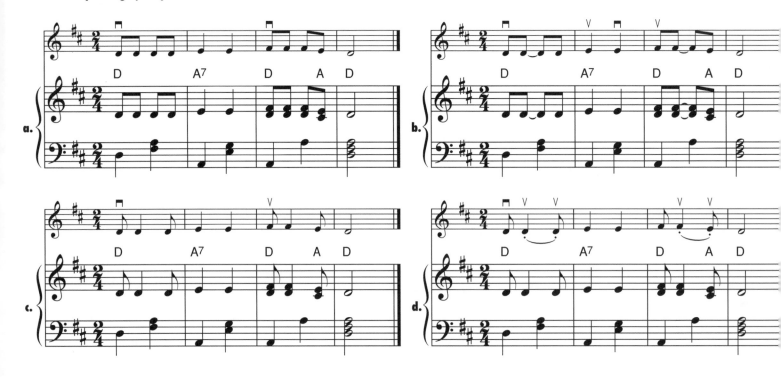

162. An Offbeat Melody

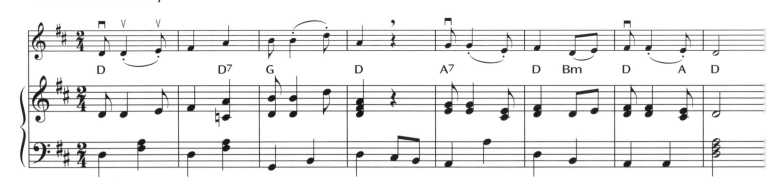

163. Mixin' It Up

Finger "Tips"

164. Exploring B♭ on the A String

165. Exploring B♭ on the G String

166. Further Exploration

167. Exploring the F Major Scale

168. Exploring Arpeggios

169. Exploring Thirds

Putting It **Together**

170. The Syncopated Piper

Variation on an Irish Folk Song

171. Shoo Fly

African-American Folk Song

172. Click Your Heels

Polish Folk Song

73. Tango (Duet)

74. Hornpipe

George Frideric Handel (1685–1759)

EXPLORING THE CONTEMPORARY ERA

Terra Nova

Richard Meyer (1957–

ACTIVITY PAGE 5

Exploring Music Theory: Shepherd's Hey

(In augmentation)

Exploring Ear Training

Exploring Improvisation: Bile Them Cabbage Down

Exploring World Music: Bridal March from Valdres

EXPLORING THE BLUES

75. Arco's Blues

Bob Phillips (1953–)

EXPLORING SOLOS

La Rejouissance (from *Royal Fireworks Music*)

George Frideric Handel (1685–175
Arr. by Richard Mey

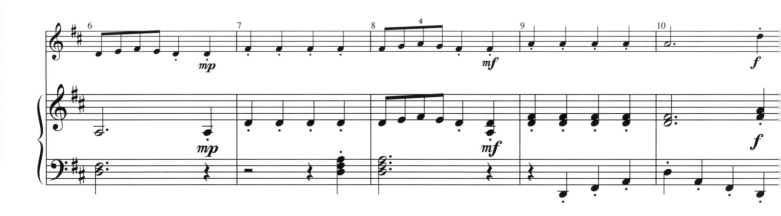

EXPLORING SOLOS

Minuet

Georg Philipp Telemann (1681–176
Arr. by Richard Me

EXPLORING SOLOS

March in G

J. S. Bach (1685–1750)
Arr. by Richard Meyer

EXPLORING SOLOS

Musette

J. S. Bach (1685–175
Arr. by Richard Mey

FUTURE FRONTIERS

176. Sailing the High Seas

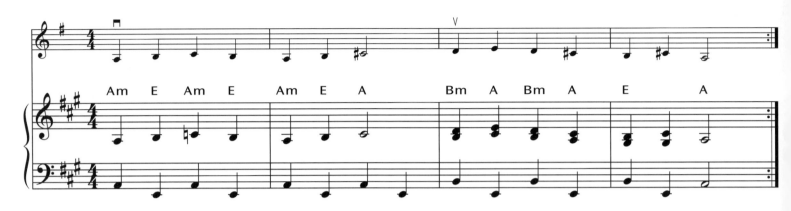

177. Exploring G#

178. Exploring the A Major Scale

179. French Folk Song

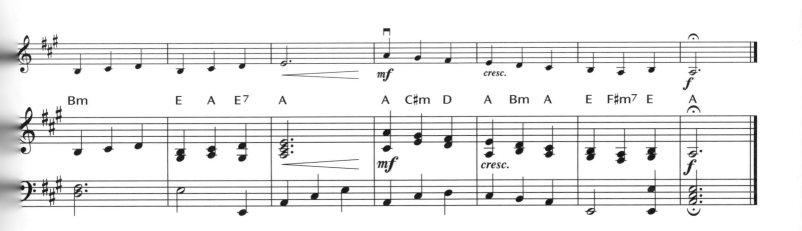